THIS BOOK BELONGS to:
_____

ISBN: 979-8-218-86750-8
Cover and illustrations by Beatriz McDonald
Published by Aletheia Theology
Printed in the United States of America
First edition

Dog Asks God

-The Creation Story-

Written by: Kait Jones

Illustrated by: Beatriz McDonald

It was dawn.

A new day.

Dog asked God,

"Did you make the day?"

"Yes, Dog,"
said God,

" I made

day

and

light,

dark
and
night."

Genesis 1:3-5

Dog went on a walk.

He saw the

sky.

Dog asked God,

"Did you make the sky?"

"Yes, Dog,"
said God,

"I made it

v a s t

and

blue.

I made the clouds, too!"

Genesis 1:8

Next,

Dog went to the pond.

He got in.

Dog asked God,

"Did you m

this

"I did," said God.

"I made all water
and all land:

from pond and swamp,
to mud and sand."

Genesis 1:9-10

Dog left the pond.
He sat on a dirt path.
He saw flowers.

Dog asked God,

"Did you make flowers?"

God said,
"Yes, Dog.

I made all plants:
flowers,
trees,
grass,
and weeds."

Genesis 1:11-13

The sun had almost set.

The moon and stars
were up.

Dog asked God,
"Did you make those?"

"Yes, Dog," said God.

"I made the sun, the moon,
and all the stars...

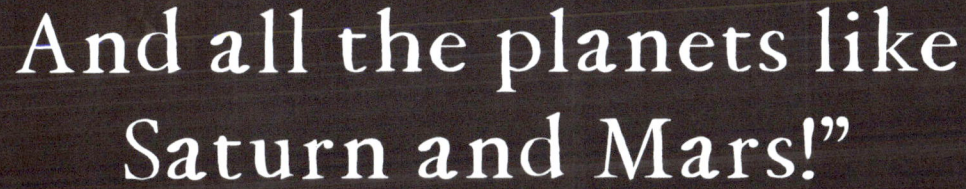

And all the planets like
Saturn and Mars!"

Genesis 1:14-19

Dog kept on.
He saw a bird.

Dog asked God,
"Did you make that bird?"

"Yes, Dog," said God,
"I made birds and cats,
pigs and rats,
foxes, frogs,
fish and fawns!
I made all animals,
even you!"

Genesis 1:20-25

It got dark.
Dog ran home.
He saw his family.

Dog asked God,
"Did you make them, too?"

"Yes, Dog," said God.
"I made humans to
watch over you."

Genesis 1:26-31

Dog got in bed.

He had to rest.

Dog asked God,
"Did you make rest?"

God said,
"Yes, Dog, I made rest.
Rest well, Dog, for it is
blessed."

Dog pondered all that God
said as he fell asleep on his bed.

Genesis 2:1-3

To my children:

May you grow in love & knowledge of the One who made you in His image.

   I love you infinitely... and God loves you the MOST!

www.ingramcontent.com/pod-product-compliance
Lightning Source LLC
Chambersburg PA
CBHW041558120626
46551CB00002B/255